The Embodied Rosary

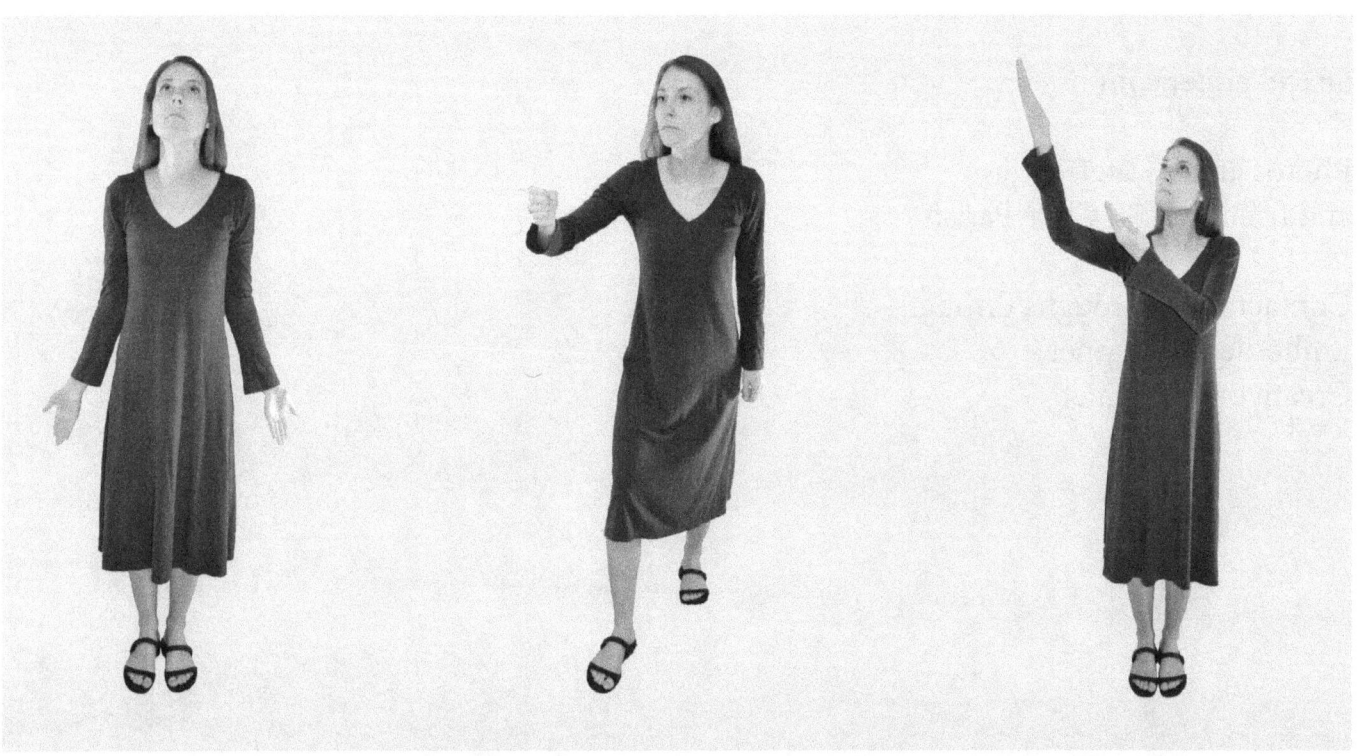

Entering the Mysteries through Gestures
By J. Thomas Sparough and Geralyn Hoxsey Sparough

The Embodied Rosary
Entering the Mysteries through Gestures
Original Copyright 2014 by J. Thomas Sparough and Geralyn Hoxsey Sparough
Second Edition Copyright 2016
All rights reserved
ISBN # 978-0-9772902-4-6

Space Painter Publications
4228 Delaney Street
Cincinnati, OH 45223
(513) 542-1231

SpacePainter.com

Photos are of Kateri Gries
and friends of St. Clare Parish

Contact the Sparoughs through
EmbodiedRosary.net
Creative-Retreat.net

RESCRIPT

In accord with the *Code of Canon Law*, I hereby grant the *Imprimatur* ("Permission to Publish") regarding the manuscript entitled *The Embodied Rosary*.

> Most Reverend Joseph R. Binzer
> Auxiliary Bishop
> Vicar General
> Archdiocese of Cincinnati
> Cincinnati, Ohio
> November 30, 2016

The *Imprimatur* ("Permission to Publish") is a declaration that a book or pamphlet is considered to be free of doctrinal or moral error. It is not implied that those who have granted the *Imprimatur* agree with the contents, opinions or statements expressed.

Table of Contents

Opening
Dedication 5
The Story of the Embodied Rosary 6
How to Use this Book 8
Traditional Days for Praying the Mysteries 9
The Embodied Rosary in 12 Steps 10
The Embodied Rosary Prayer 10

Prayers of the Holy Rosary
The Sign of the Cross 11
The Apostles' Creed 11
The Our Father 12
The Hail Mary 12
The Glory Be 13
The Fatima Prayer 14
The Hail Holy Queen 14
Let Us Pray 15

The Embodied Rosary
The Joyful Mysteries 16
The Luminous Mysteries 22
The Sorrowful Mysteries 28
The Glorious Mysteries 34

Appendix
Expanded Hail Mary Gestures 40
Scripture References 41

About the Authors 43

Dedication

We dedicate the Embodied Rosary to St. John Bosco, Patron Saint of Youth. His teachings continue to inspire us. He made our faith engaging, approachable, understandable, and even fun. We strive to do the same. Because of St. John Bosco, we know that Mary, Help of Christians is our guide.

"Run, jump, play, but do not sin."

"Be devoted to Mary, Help of Christians and you will see what miracles are!"

> --St. John Bosco

The Origin of the Embodied Rosary

It was a moment of the Holy Spirit.

Praying the Rosary with my religious education class was a challenge. My 7th-8th grade students were slowly disintegrating as we were making our way through the sorrowful mysteries.

The kids were trying to be respectful, yet they were disengaged from the prayer, yawning, burping, minds wandering, pinned to their seats, and their bodies saying, "When will this be over?"

An idea flashed through my mind. We were on "The Carrying of the Cross." I told the kids to stand up, pick up their chairs, and put them over their shoulders. They laughed nervously and asked, "Seriously?"

I said, "Yes, pick up your chair, as if it is the cross, and you are Jesus."

They picked up their chairs, and we launched into our next Hail Mary. Now, they were engaged. I had them keep the chairs over their shoulders for several Hail Marys.

When we got to the crucifixion, I had them put their arms out, as if nailed to the cross. We alternated this gesture with simply standing as we proceeded through the decade.

Those changes transformed the Rosary experience for the kids and for me. It helped us to enter into the story. It was enlightening, engaging, prayerful, and, dare I say it, even fun.

I brought that idea home to my wife, Geralyn, a long-time dancer, youth minister and teacher. We let go of picking up chairs, but together we shaped that Holy Spirit moment into the Embodied Rosary.

J. Thomas Sparough

"The greatest method of praying is to pray the Rosary."
   --St. Francis de Sales

"There is nothing to stop children and young people from praying the Rosary – either within the family or in groups – with appropriate symbolic and practical aids to understanding and appreciation."

   --St. John Paul II
       Rosarium Virginis Mariae

What is the Embodied Rosary?

The Embodied Rosary is a method to pray the Rosary. It uses symbolic gestures as a practical aid to illuminate the mysteries. Each gesture is held for two Hail Marys, first as a physical prompt to help imaginatively enter into the scripture scene, and second to help us reflect on our own life in terms of that scripture scene. To assist us in this process, there is a brief description or question with each Hail Mary. The connecting prayers, e.g Our Father, Glory Be, have basic gestures that remain consistent throughout the Rosary. Using this experiential method, participants literally and figuratively embody the story.

Why Pray the Embodied Rosary?

Even those who find great value in the Rosary may have trouble concentrating on the mysteries. The Embodied Rosary uses a physical prompt to connect participants to the scripture scenes found in the mysteries. For many, this transforms the Rosary into a reflective, intimate journey with Our Lord and Our Lady. For many youth, it makes the prayer understandable and engaging.

Are Rosary Beads No Longer Needed?

When praying the Embodied Rosary, most people find it easier to not use their beads. This allows a fuller entry into the gestures. However, some people like to use their beads. We are not suggesting that the Embodied Rosary replace the traditional method of praying the Rosary. This beloved prayer with beads gives comfort and strength to millions.

Is this the same as the Living Rosary?

No, the two are much different, but complementary. The Living Rosary uses a person to represent each bead of the Rosary. That person stands up, or lights a candle, or leads the Hail Mary or Our Father when it is his or her turn. That action is successively performed by one person at a time. In this way, the beads of the Rosary are actually living people.

In contrast, when praying the Embodied Rosary everyone joins in each gesture for every Hail Mary, as well as all the connecting prayers. In this way, it is much more physically inclusive and participatory for all involved. And, most importantly, the gestures in the Embodied Rosary are physical prompts for entering more deeply into the scripture story related to each of the mysteries.

Who is the Embodied Rosary For?

It is for everyone who wants to pray the Rosary, and an engaging tool for those who would rather not. The Embodied Rosary is not meant to replace the traditional way to pray the Rosary, but offers a new experience to enhance anyone's prayer life. It is especially appropriate for children, grandparents, and whole families. Since it slows the Rosary down and helps one to enter into the stories, it is a useful tool for adults looking for contemplative prayer.

Do I have to Use these Gestures?

To experience the Embodied Rosary, we invite you to use these gestures that we feel reflect the mysteries of the Holy Rosary. The gestures shown here are not absolutes. They are our artistic representation of the scripture stories. It can be quite moving to adapt or create your own gestures based on your personal connection to the scripture scenes.

Praying the Embodied Rosary for Others

While the reflection questions listed in this book are mostly presented in the first person, many of us pray the Rosary with the intention of helping others. Feel free to explore beyond the written questions of this book and adapt the contemplations as the Spirit guides you. Images of loved ones or those in need may be evoked by the scripture itself, and this is a wonderful opportunity to bring their concerns to prayer. Feel free to let your heart lead you as you turn your concerns over to Christ and his Mother of Mercy.

How to use this Booklet

--For Private Prayer

Use this booklet as a script for praying the Embodied Rosary. As you become familiar with the gestures and meditations, the script might even be set aside. It is not doing the gestures exactly, and reading the descriptions perfectly, that is most important. It is not how high your hand is raised, or which foot is forward that matters. What matters is imagining yourself in the story. The gestures and descriptions merely set the stage. It is up to you to enter the scene. Pray for help. Mary will be your guide.

If you have limited mobility, are seated in a chair, or confined to a bed, do these gestures in any way you are able. A tilt of the head, or changing your hand position, may be all you need to feel like you are entering the mysteries.

--For the Group Leader

Everything we have said about private prayer also applies to group settings.

Although not always possible, it is helpful to have two people lead, one for the gestures and the other for the verbal descriptions and prayers. (Note: The person reading the descriptions should also join in the gestures.) It works well to have a number of assigned individuals help lead, taking turns showing gestures, reading the descriptions and prayers.

The leader has other choices. For instance, we have included here the Fatima Prayer. This prayer is optional. We like to include a cycle of gestures for the first three Hail Marys (see appendix). Some leaders might add in a brief song verse after the Glory Be, such as the Ave Maria chorus. Other leaders might create opportunities for participants to name intentions at the beginning of the Rosary and/or each decade.

To become familiar with this embodied method of praying the Rosary, look through this guide; try out the gestures. Photography limits this to a series of static gestures, but we find that the movement the leader models to get into each of the gestures is powerful, especially during the mysteries. You will be exploring different characters, energy, emotions, and relationships as part of your prayer. **Every gesture has movement getting into it.** A book can't adequately convey this. Experiment to find what motions work for you.

Practice the prayer form, so that as a leader, you feel comfortable embodying the gestures and stances with conviction and energy. Some moments are deep and sorrowful; others are light or even playful. You may find your voice changing, along with your facial expressions, as you embody the fullness of the mysteries. That is good. Your expression and commitment will help give permission to others trying this for the first time. This method takes time, but because the story takes over, we also find it passes quickly.

If you have room, you may invite participants to gather in a circle. But that is not necessary. The Embodied Rosary works in church pews, classrooms, gymnasiums, cars, and paths in the woods, to name a few of the places we've shared it.

Acknowledgements

We want to thank all those who helped make this method of praying the Rosary a reality. Thank you to Steve Sparough, Michael Sparough, S.J., Tria and George O'Maille, Joan and Michael Hoxsey, Bobby Fisher, our children Kateri and Joseph, our friends at St. Clare Parish, other siblings, cousins, nieces, nephews, and many friends who helped us.

A special thank you to Betsey Beckman. Her inspiration brought this method into existence. Her guidance refined it. And her enthusiasm enlivened it!

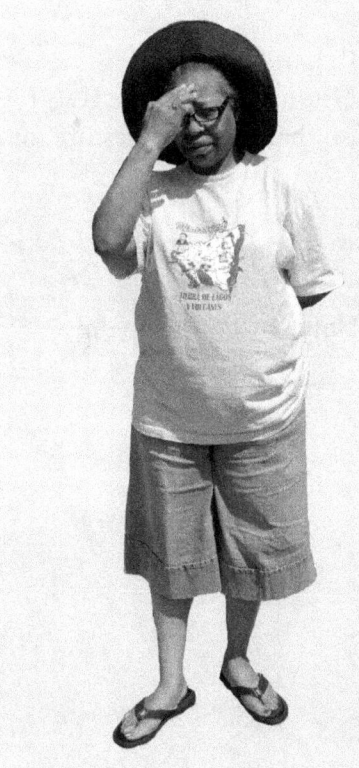

"The power of the Rosary is beyond description."
   --Venerable Fulton J. Sheen

"We pray the Rosary even in the streets."
   --Blessed Teresa of Calcutta

"The family that prays together stays together."
   --Fr. Patrick Peyton

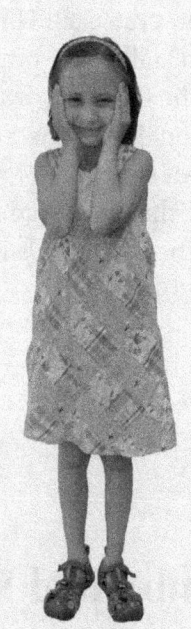

Traditional Days for Praying the Mysteries

Joyful Mysteries—Mondays and Saturdays; Sundays of Christmas Season

The Annunciation--The Visitation--The Nativity--The Presentation in the Temple--The Finding in the Temple

Luminous Mysteries—Thursdays

The Baptism in the Jordan--The Wedding Feast at Cana--The Proclamation of the Kingdom of God--The Transfiguration--The Institution of the Eucharist

Sorrowful Mysteries—Tuesdays and Fridays; Sundays in Lent

The Agony in the Garden--The Scourging at the Pillar--The Crowning of Thorns--The Carrying of the Cross--The Crucifixion

Glorious Mysteries—Wednesdays and Sundays

The Resurrection--The Ascension--The Descent of the Holy Spirit--The Assumption--
The Coronation

The Embodied Rosary in 12 Steps

1. Say the Embodied Rosary Prayer with hands together, palms up.
2. Make and say the Sign of the Cross.
3. Say the Apostles' Creed with hand over heart.
4. Say an Our Father with hands clasped.
5. Say the Hail Mary three times following the gestures listed on page 12 or 40.
6. Say the Glory Be with palms outstretched.
7. Announce the first mystery, read the reflection, and say the Our Father with hands clasped.
8. Starting with number one, embody the gesture, read the description or question, and hold the gesture as you pray each Hail Mary. Note that the cycle of five gestures is repeated so that there is a gesture for all 10 Hail Mary prayers.
9. Say the Glory Be with palms outstretched.
10. Optional - say the Fatima Prayer with fist over heart.
11. Repeat steps 7-10 for the 2nd, 3rd, 4th, and 5th mysteries.
12. After the five decades are completed, finish the Rosary saying the a) Hail, Holy Queen with palms together; b) Let Us Pray with hands open; and c) the Sign of the Cross.

The Embodied Rosary Prayer

Mother Mary
Take us by the hand
Through your Holy Rosary.
Reveal the life of Jesus
As only you can tell it.

So that
His joy might be our joy.
His light might be our light.
His sorrow might be our sorrow.
And His glory might be our glory.

Now and forever,
Amen.

Hands together, palms up while saying this prayer.

The Sign of the Cross

In the name of the Father

And of the Son

And of the Holy

Spirit

Amen.

The Apostles' Creed

I believe in God, the Father almighty, Creator of heaven and earth. And in Jesus Christ, His only Son, our Lord, who was conceived by the Holy Spirit, born of the Virgin Mary, suffered under Pontius Pilate, was crucified, died, and was buried. He descended into hell; on the third day He rose again from the dead. He ascended into heaven, and is seated at the right hand of God the Father Almighty; from there He will come to judge the living and the dead. I believe in the Holy Spirit, the Holy Catholic Church, the communion of saints, the forgiveness of sins, the resurrection of the body, and life everlasting.

Amen

Hand over heart while saying the Apostles' Creed.

The Our Father

Our Father who art in heaven, hallowed be Thy name; Thy kingdom come; Thy will be done on earth as it is in heaven. Give us this day our daily bread; and forgive us our trespasses as we forgive those who trespass against us; and lead us not into temptation, but deliver us from evil.

Amen

Note that only the leader says the sections that are bolded, as is typically done when praying the Rosary in a group. We also say this prayer at the start of each decade, just after the mystery announcement, and scripture story description.

Hold tightly to the Lord as you say the Our Father.

The Hail Mary

Hail Mary, full of grace, the Lord is with thee. Blessed art thou among women, and blessed is the fruit of thy womb, Jesus.

Holy Mary, Mother of God, pray for us sinners, now and at the hour of our death.

Amen

This prayer is the heart of the Rosary and is said three times in the introduction and 10 times in each decade. Each of these three gestures is used for one Hail Mary in the introduction. Try tracing the sign of the cross over your heart, lips and mind just before the Hail Mary. Refer to the mystery segments of this book for the gestures to be used in each decade.

Say: May these words be ever on our heart.

Say: May these words be ever on our lips

Say: May these words be ever on our minds.

Another option for the first three Hail Marys is to use the complete cycle of gestures found in the appendix on page 40. In that option, there is a gesture for every phrase of the prayer. This can be useful as it gives special focus to the prayer itself, which is perfect for the introduction. In the decades, the focus of the gestures will be on the scriptural stories of the mysteries.

The Glory Be

**Glory be
To the Father
And to the Son
And to the Holy Spirit;**
As it was in the beginning, is now,
and ever shall be, world without end.

Amen

Arms open in praise as you say the Glory Be.

This prayer completes the introduction. It is also said at the end of each decade, just before the popular, but optional, Fatima Prayer.

The Fatima Prayer

Oh my Jesus, forgive us our sins, save us from the fires of hell, lead all souls to heaven, especially those in most need of Thy mercy.

If chosen, say this optional prayer after the Glory Be at the end of each decade, but not in the introductory prayers.

Fist over heart as you say the Fatima Prayer.

The Hail Holy Queen

Hail, Holy Queen, Mother of mercy, our life, our sweetness, and our hope! To thee do we cry, poor banished children of Eve. To thee do we send up our sighs, mourning and weeping in this valley of tears. Turn then, most gracious advocate, thine eyes of mercy towards us, and after this our exile, show unto us the blessed fruit of thy womb, Jesus. O clement, O loving, O sweet Virgin Mary. **Pray for us, O holy Mother of God,** that we may be made worthy of the promises of Christ.

Hands folded as you say the Hail Holy Queen.

As one of two concluding prayers, this prayer is only said once in the entire Rosary.

Let Us Pray

Let us pray, O God, whose only begotten Son, by His life, death, and resurrection, has purchased for us the rewards of eternal life; grant we beseech Thee, that meditating on these mysteries of the most Holy Rosary of the Blessed Virgin Mary, we may imitate what they contain, and obtain what they promise. Through the same Christ Our Lord.

Amen

This prayer is only said once and is the final prayer in the Rosary. Complete the Embodied Rosary with the **Sign of the Cross.**

Hands open as you say the Let Us Pray.

"Praying the Rosary together, as a family, is very beautiful and a source of great strength!"

--Pope Francis

The Joyful Mysteries

Decade Instructions for the Embodied Rosary

- Announce the mystery and read the reflection.
- Pray the Our Father with your hands clasped together.
- Starting with number one, make the gesture, read the description or question, and hold the gesture as you pray the Hail Mary. Repeat this process for 2-10.
- Finish with the Glory Be and Fatima Prayer.

- For complete instructions and prayers see page 10.

All participants embody the gesture for each Hail Mary

The First Joyful Mystery

The Annunciation

The Angel Gabriel announces to Mary that she is greatly favored by God. Mary is startled and troubled, but Gabriel tells her not to be afraid, for God has chosen her to bear a Son, whom she will call Jesus. The angel assures Mary that with God all things are possible. Mary agrees to God's plan, calling herself a handmaid of the Lord.

1. Gabriel comes to Mary with wings out-stretched in angelic glory.

2. Who are the angels in my life?

3. Mary is startled and in fear of Gabriel.

4. When have I been startled?

5. Gabriel comforts Mary, and explains God's plan.

6. Whom am I called to comfort?

7. Mary contemplates God's request.

8. What is God asking of me?

9. Mary accepts God's request and says, "Yes!" to God's plan.

10. What "yes" am I willing to give?

The Second Joyful Mystery

The Visitation

Mary sets out to visit her cousin Elizabeth, who is now pregnant even in her old age, because nothing is impossible with God. When Elizabeth hears Mary's greeting, the babe in her womb leaps for joy. Elizabeth calls Mary "most blessed." Mary is filled with awe and joy when she sees Elizabeth. Mary proclaims the greatness of the Lord in the Magnificat.

1. Elizabeth, elderly and six months pregnant, looks to see who has arrived.

2. How have I experienced an answer to long-held prayers?

3. Mary with hands over her womb, waits for Elizabeth.

4. How have I helped family members in need?

5. Elizabeth greets Mary, while her son John leaps for joy in her womb.

6. How do I see God working in others?

7. Mary is overcome with all that she has heard and seen.

8. When have I been overcome by joy?

9. Mary praises the Lord in Heaven. Her soul proclaims the greatness of the Lord.

10. How do I glorify God?

The Third Joyful Mystery

The Nativity

Joseph takes Mary to Bethlehem for the census, but there is no room at the inn. Joseph pleads with the innkeeper for shelter. Mary gives birth to Jesus. Angels announce to shepherds that the Messiah is born. After visiting the infant they glorify and praise God. A star of great brilliance also announces Jesus' birth.

1. The innkeeper decisively states there is no room.

2. When have I closed my heart to the needs of others?

3. Joseph pleads with the innkeeper for shelter for Mary.

4. How have I been an advocate for the poor and marginalized?

5. Mary takes the first look into the eyes of the living God, Jesus.

6. When have I seen the face of God in a child?

7. With crook in hand, the shepherds shout the good news. "The Savior is born!"

8. Have I spread the Good News joyfully?

9. The guiding star shines brightly for all to see.

10. What is the guiding light in my life?

The Fourth Joyful Mystery

The Presentation

Mary and Joseph take Jesus to the Temple to fulfill the law. A holy man named Simeon, and an aged prophetess named Anna, joyfully recognize Jesus as the Messiah. Simeon takes Jesus into his arms and blesses God for revealing the Savior to him, but he tells Mary that a sword of sorrrow will pierce her heart.

1. Simeon strokes his long beard as he spots Jesus.

2. What has God promised me?

3. Anna caresses her knuckles in prayer as she notices the Holy Family.

4. When have I waited for something that took a long time to arrive?

5. Simeon and Anna rejoice that the Savior is in their midst.

6. Do I remember to give thanks and celebrate when my prayers are answered?

7. Mary hands the baby Jesus over to Simeon to hold.

8. What is my offering to God?

9. Mary holds Jesus protectively when told a sword will pierce her heart.

10. How have I been pierced by the sword of sorrow?

The Fifth Joyful Mystery

The Finding in the Temple

After the Passover Feast, when Jesus is 12, he remains in Jerusalem without Mary and Joseph knowing. After a three-day search, they return to Jerusalem and find him in the Temple listening and asking questions. The elders are astounded by Jesus' understanding of the scriptures. Mary's relief at finding Jesus surprises him.

1. Joseph shrugs, not knowing Jesus' whereabouts.

2. When have I experienced being separated from one of my loved ones?

3. Mary shields her eyes as she searches for Jesus.

4. What have I been searching for in my relationship with God?

5. Jesus listens to and questions the teachers in the Temple.

6. What questions do I have for the leaders of my faith?

7. The elders are astounded by Jesus' understanding of the scriptures.

8. Have I learned something from someone I did not expect to impress me?

9. Mary embraces Jesus in relief.

10. How have I experienced finding someone who was lost?

The Luminous Mysteries

Decade Instructions for the Embodied Rosary

- Announce the mystery and read the reflection.
- Pray the Our Father with your hands clasped together.
- Starting with number one, make the gesture, read the description or question, and hold the gesture as you pray the Hail Mary. Repeat this process for 2-10.
- Finish with the Glory Be and Fatima Prayer.

- For complete instructions and prayers see page 10.

All participants embody the gesture for each Hail Mary

The First Luminous Mystery

The Baptism in the Jordan

John the Baptist is preaching and telling everyone to make straight the path of the Lord! Jesus comes to John to be baptized. John does not feel worthy to baptize Jesus, but he does as Jesus requests. The Holy Spirit appears like a dove and descends upon Jesus as a voice comes from the heavens saying, "You are my beloved Son."

1. John cries out, "Prepare the way of the Lord."

2. What have I done to prepare the way of the Lord?

3. John preaches, "Make straight the Lord's path."

4. What things in my life do I need to set straight?

5. John cups water in his hands, preparing to baptize Jesus.

6. When have I felt unworthy to do something Jesus wants me to do?

7. Jesus is baptized by John.

8. How do I live out the promises of my baptism?

9. The dove descends from Heaven to rest on Jesus.

10. What are signs of God's love I have seen in my life?

The Second Luminous Mystery

The Wedding at Cana

Jesus and some of his disciples attend a wedding in Cana with Mary, his mother. When the wine runs out, Mary tells Jesus. He asks what she would have him do. Mary tells the servants to do whatever Jesus says. The servants fill six large jars with water. The headwaiter tastes the water that has become wine and is impressed by its quality.

1. Mary contemplates telling Jesus to help with the wine shortage.

2. Who is prompting me to do something new?

3. Jesus shrugs his shoulders, "What do you want me to do?"

4. When have I been reluctant to take action?

5. Mary directs the servants to do whatever Jesus tells them to do.

6. What instructions does Mary give to me?

7. A servant fills a large stone jar with water as directed by Jesus.

8. How have I contributed to something bigger than I expected?

9. The headwaiter tasting the new wine is surprised by its excellent quality.

10. What wonderful surprise have I experienced in my life?

The Third Luminous Mystery

The Proclamation of the Kingdom of God

Jesus says the kingdom of God is at hand and shares the Good News with all who will listen. He says turn away from revenge and toward compassion. Jesus describes the kingdom as a tiny mustard seed that grows large enough to provide shelter. Also, Jesus tells us that unless we welcome the kingdom like a child, we will not enter it.

1. Jesus declares the kingdom of God is at hand.

2. How do I proclaim the kingdom of God?

3. Jesus proclaims that the kingdom of Heaven belongs to the poor in spirit.

4. How do I feel blessed?

5. Jesus teaches us not to demand an eye for an eye, but to turn the other cheek.

6. Have I been able to turn the other cheek?

7. Jesus says the kingdom of God is like a tiny mustard seed.

8. How have I experienced my faith growing like a mustard seed?

9. Jesus tells us we must be like a child in order to enter the kindgom of God.

10. What does it mean to me to welcome the kingdom of God like a child?

The Fourth Luminous Mystery

The Transfiguration

Jesus leads Peter, James and John up a mountain. Jesus is transfigured before them; he shines like the sun. Elijah and Moses appear, and Peter offers to set up three tents. A bright cloud shadows the group, and God's voice says, "This is my beloved Son, with whom I am well pleased; listen to him." The frightened disciples fall to the ground. Jesus, touching them, tells them not to be afraid.

1. Jesus, using a walking stick, leads Peter, John and James up the mountain.

2. What mountaintop experiences have I had?

3. Jesus is transfigured, shining bright as the sun.

4. Is Jesus the light of my world?

5. Peter offers to build three tents.

6. How have I extended hospitality to others?

7. The disciples cower in fear when they hear the voice of God.

8. How able am I to listen, and act without fear, to the voice of God in my life?

9. Jesus touching the disciples says, "Rise, and do not be afraid."

10. Have I felt Jesus encourage me to not be afraid?

The Fifth Luminous Mystery

The Institution of the Eucharist

During the Last Supper, Jesus blesses bread and wine, transforming them into his Body and Blood. In Emmaus, after the resurrection, it is in the blessing and breaking of the bread that the eyes of the disciples are opened to the presence of the risen Jesus.

1. Jesus blesses the bread during the Last Supper.

2. How do I experience the Eucharist?

3. A disciple shares in the Body of Christ.

4. How am I nourished by the Body of Christ?

5. Jesus lifts the cup as he blesses the wine.

6. Am I willing to sacrifice myself for the sake of another person?

7. A disciple drinks from the cup of the Blood of Christ.

8. Have I shared my thirst for the Lord with others?

9. A disciple in Emmaus recognizes Jesus in the breaking of the bread.

10. Do I recognize Jesus in the breaking of the bread?

The Sorrowful Mysteries

Decade Instructions for the Embodied Rosary

- Announce the mystery and read the reflection.
- Pray the Our Father with your hands clasped together.
- Starting with number one, make the gesture, read the description or question, and hold the gesture as you pray the Hail Mary. Repeat this process for 2-10.
- Finish with the Glory Be and Fatima Prayer.

- For complete instructions and prayers see page 10.

All participants embody the gesture for each Hail Mary

The First Sorrowful Mystery

The Agony in the Garden

After the Last Supper, Jesus goes to the Garden of Gethsemane to pray. Jesus asks his disciples to keep watch and pray with him, but they are not able to remain awake. Jesus prays in great distress about his future, but ultimately accepts God's will. Judas betrays him with a kiss.

1. Jesus prays that the cup of suffering may pass him by.

2. When have I asked God to let this suffering pass me by?

3. Jesus prays to the Father, "Not my will, but your will be done."

4. How open am I to accepting God's will over my own?

5. The disciples fall asleep.

6. When have I fallen asleep in my relationship with God?

7. Jesus prays in agony to the point that his sweat is like drops of blood.

8. How do I rely on God in times of agony?

9. Jesus accepts God's plan and meets his betrayer Judas with a sorrowful heart.

10. How have I betrayed Jesus through my own actions or inactions?

The Second Sorrowful Mystery

The Scourging at the Pillar

Pilate has Jesus whipped before he is sent to be crucified. Soldiers brutally carry out the punishment.

1. Jesus stands with hands tied.

2. How have I found my hands tied?

3. A soldier whips Jesus with the right hand.

4. Whom have I hurt?

5. Another soldier strikes with his left hand.

6. When have I followed rules without thought?

7. The first soldier strikes again hitting lower.

8. Whom have I continued to hurt who was already suffering?

9. The other soldier strikes lower.

10. How have I sacrificed myself for others?

The Third Sorrowful Mystery

The Crowning with Thorns

After his scourging the soldiers make a crown of thorns and push it onto Jesus' head. The soldiers bow mockingly to Jesus, "King of the Jews." They spit on him and slap him repeatedly. Mary offers her prayers to help Jesus.

1. A soldier places a crown made of thorns on Jesus' head.

2. How have I been responsible for another person's pain?

3. Jesus wears the "crown of thorns" piercing his scalp.

4. What mental burden pierces my mind?

5. A soldier bows in mockery.

6. How have I been ridiculed?

7. Another soldier slaps Jesus in the face.

8. Whom have I wanted to slap?

9. Mother Mary prays fervently for Jesus.

10. For whom am I praying?

The Fourth Sorrowful Mystery

The Carrying of the Cross

Jesus must carry his own cross on his way to his crucifixion. Tradition says that Jesus falls three times on the way to Golgotha, the Place of the Skull. A Roman soldier chooses Simon, a Cyrenian, from the crowd to help Jesus carry his cross.

1. Jesus carries the cross over his right shoulder.

2. What is my cross to bear?

3. Jesus falls.

4. When have I had to rise up after a fall?

5. Jesus shifts the cross to his other shoulder.

6. What are the global crosses that I carry?

7. Jesus falls again.

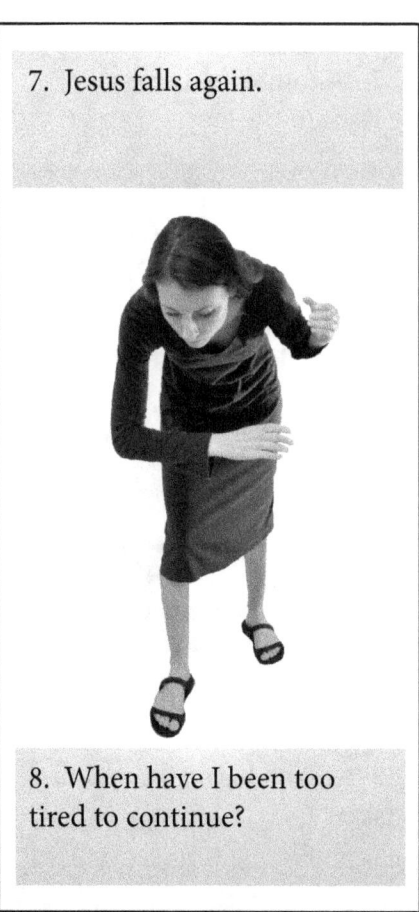

8. When have I been too tired to continue?

9. A soldier orders Simon, the Cyrene, to pick up Jesus' cross.

10. How willing am I to help others in times of need?

The Fifth Sorrowful Mystery

The Crucifixion

Jesus is nailed to the cross one arm at a time and both feet. When the soldiers finish nailing him to the cross, they place him between two thieves for all to see. His mother Mary and the disciple John remain at the foot of the cross throughout Jesus' suffering and death. He unites them as mother and son.

1. Jesus has one hand nailed to the cross.

2. Who is dying unjustly?

3. Jesus' other hand is nailed to the cross.

4. Do I feel Jesus' pain?

5. Then both feet are nailed to the cross.

6. Are my feet on the path of sacrifice and compassion?

7. Mother Mary prays at the foot of the cross and Jesus unites her and John.

8. What does Jesus say to me when I come to Him at the foot of the cross?

9. Jesus, fully crucified, says, "It is finished," and hands over his spirit.

10. For whom am I willing to die?

The Glorious Mysteries

Decade Instructions for the Embodied Rosary

- Announce the mystery and read the reflection.
- Pray the Our Father with your hands clasped together.
- Starting with number one, make the gesture, read the description or question, and hold the gesture as you pray the Hail Mary. Repeat this process for 2-10.
- Finish with the Glory Be and Fatima Prayer.

- For complete instructions and prayers see page 10.

All participants embody the gesture for each Hail Mary

The First Glorious Mystery

The Resurrection

Mary Magdalene, startled by an earthquake, an angel, and the empty tomb, runs to tell the disciples. Peter and John hurry back to the tomb. Mary Magdalene meets Christ in the garden and reaches out to touch him. Jesus appears to the disciples blessing them with peace. Thomas finally believes when he sees and touches Jesus' wounds.

1. Mary Magdalene is startled at the empty tomb.

2. When have I been amazed?

3. Mary runs to tell the disciples. Peter and John run back to the tomb.

4. When have I had news I couldn't wait to share?

5. Mary Magdalene reaches out to touch the risen Christ.

6. When have I reached out to Jesus?

7. Jesus appears to the disciples, "Peace be with you."

8. Do I feel the peace that Jesus offers in this moment?

9. Thomas touches the wounds of Jesus and says, "My Lord and my God."

10. What doubts do I struggle with?

The Second Glorious Mystery

The Ascension

Prior to his ascension, Jesus asks Peter if he loves him. Peter confirms his love for Jesus three times as Jesus tells him, "Feed my sheep." Jesus blesses his disciples before ascending to Heaven. He tells them to go and make disciples of all nations.

1. Jesus, speaking from the heart, asks Simon Peter, "Do you love me?"

2. What question does Jesus ask me?

3. Peter responds, "Yes Lord, you know that I love you."

4. How do I answer the question Jesus asks me?

5. Jesus tells Peter, "Feed my sheep."

6. How does my love for Jesus translate into my actions in the world?

7. Jesus blesses his disciples and tells them to go and make disciples of all nations.

8. Do I feel Jesus' blessing?

9. Jesus ascends to Heaven.

10. How do I imagine that glorious day of Jesus' Ascension?

The Third Glorious Mystery

The Descent of the Holy Spirit

The Holy Spirit descends as tongues of fire upon Jesus' followers. Filled with the Holy Spirit they are able to speak in many languages. Visitors from many different countries are confused that they can understand the disciples. Peter proclaims Jesus' life, death and resurrection as the fulfillment of scripture. About 3,000 people convert to be followers of Christ this day.

1. The Holy Spirit descends on the disciples as tongues of fire.

2. How have I experienced the Holy Spirit entering my life?

3. The Holy Spirit pours out of the disciples in many languages.

4. What has the Holy Spirit empowered me to do?

5. Visitors are bewildered to hear their own language proclaimed by the disciples.

6. What don't I understand about my faith?

7. Peter confidently addresses the crowd.

8. How have I been inspired to speak up?

9. Thousands raise their hands to join the Apostles.

10. Would I be among the 3,000 who joined the apostles that day?

© J. Thomas Sparough 2016 Embodied Rosary more information and video at EmbodiedRosary.net

The Fourth Glorious Mystery

The Assumption

We imagine, as she approaches death, Mary reflects on pivitol events in her life. Gabriel's visit, Jesus's birth and death are significant in her memory. Church teaching states that Mary was taken into Heaven body and soul when the course of her earthy life was finished. Her Son welcomes her in Heaven.

1. Mary recalls the Angel Gabriel's announcement.

2. Whom will I remember at the end of my life?

3. Mary recollects the arrival and cradling of the baby Jesus in her arms.

4. What memories of new beginnings stand out for me?

5. Mary remembers the pain of Jesus' crucifixion.

6. What is something painful in my life that I will never forget?

7. Mary takes her last breath on earth.

8. How am I preparing for my own death?

9. Mary is welcomed to Heaven with an embrace from Jesus.

10. Whom do I long to embrace in Heaven?

The Fifth Glorious Mystery

The Coronation

As the mother of Jesus, the King of Kings, Mary is crowned Queen of Heaven and Angels. We can call on her and she intercedes for us through many manifestations.

1. Jesus crowns his mother Mary Queen of Heaven and Angels.

2. How do I show honor to the Queen of Heaven?

3. Mary, Queen of Peace, wears her crown.

4. How do I help create peace for myself and others?

5. Mary intercedes for us as Mother of Mercy, and Our Lady of Perpetual Help.

6. Do I join Mother Mary in offering mercy to others?

7.. Our Lady of Sorrows, knows all our pain.

8. What sorrow do I carry?

9. Our Lady of Grace and Mary, Help of Christians blesses us with her love.

10. What help do I ask of Mother Mary this day?

Appendix

Expanded Hail Mary Gestures by Phrase

Scripture References

The Joyful Mysteries

Annunciation Luke 1:36-38	**Visitation** Luke 1:39-55	**Nativity** Luke 2:1-20 Matthew 2:1-2	**Presentation of the Lord** Luke 2:22-38	**Finding in the Temple** Luke 2:41-52

The Luminous Mysteries

Baptism in the Jordan Matthew 3:3, 15-17	**Wedding at Cana** John 2:4-10	**Proclamation of the Kingdom** Mark 1:15; 4:30-32; 10:14-16 Matthew 5:3-12, 38-39	**Transfiguration** Luke 9:28-36 Matthew 17:1-8 Mark 9:2-8	**Institution of the Eucharist** Luke 22:19-20 Matthew 26:27 Luke 24:30-31

The Sorrowful Mysteries

Agony in the Garden Matthew 26:36-50 Luke 22:39-48 John 18:1-3	**Scourging at the Pillar** Matthew 27:26 Mark 15:15 John 19:1	**Crowning with Thorns** Matthew 27:27-31 Mark 15:16-20 John 19:2-3	**Carrying of the Cross** John 19:17 Matthew 27:32 Mark 15:21 Luke 23:26	**Crucifixion** Matthew 27:35-56 Mark 15:24-41 Luke 23:33-49 John 19:18-30

The Glorious Mysteries

Resurrection Matthew 28:1-8 Mark 16:1-6, 8 Luke 24:1-9, 36 John 20:1-4, 17, 19, 24-29	**Ascension** Matthew 28:16-2 Luke 24:50-51 John 21:15-17 Acts 1:2, 9-11	**Descent of the Holy Spirit** Acts 2:2-12, 14-41	**Assumption** *Munificentissimus Deus* Catechism of the Catholic Church, Paragraphs 966 and 2853.	**Coronation** Revelation 12:1 *Ad Caeli Reginam* Catechism of the Catholic Church, Paragraph 966.

About the Authors

Tom and Geralyn Sparough are co-founders of Creative Retreat, LLC. Besides their church work, they specialize in team building for non-profits. Based in Cincinnati, OH, USA, they travel the world sharing their creative programing.

The Sparoughs are also the authors of *The Secret Diary of Mother Mary*; and *The Spiritual Exercises of the Coffee Filter*.

For information about training in the Embodied Rosary method, and information about their books, and Creative Retreat, LLC, and for supplemental resources for the Embodied Rosary, including video teaching the gestures, visit:

EmbodiedRosary.net
Creative-Retreat.net
or call (513) 542-1231

Geralyn Hoxsey Sparough
J. Thomas Sparough

www.ingramcontent.com/pod-product-compliance
Lightning Source LLC
Chambersburg PA
CBHW060520300426
44112CB00017B/2737